TAROT AND SEX

Erotic meaning of 78 cards !

by Magdalene Aleece

ISBN : 9781099324345

Table of Contents

Introduction -5

Major Arcana - 7

Minor Arcana- Wands - 29

Minor Arcana – Swords - 43

Minor Arcana – Cups - 57

Minor Arcana – Pentacles -71

Spreads -85

Introduction

Sometimes it happens that we want to find out about details of our sex life. We ask our cards:
If there will be sex with our new admirer?
What kind of lover is he?
What we can expect in bedroom?
Will he take the initiative?

It is not easy to determine in detail what our sex life will be, the most important here is an experience, our own observations and the deck of cards we are using. There are special decks with erotic scenes and we can use them for such type of readings.
But what to do if we do not have such a deck and we want to ask what is awaiting us?
Let's use the general meaning of the cards and adjust to the situation, what tells you your intuition when you look at The Hermit, does he look like a good lover ? Pay attention to the symbols and details on your Tarot deck, do you see the water on the card? Think what it can show, a sex near the water or maybe this looks for you like a mirror? Do you see you and your lover making love in front of big mirror? First of all we should listen to our intuition and often meditate with cards. When we choose a specific card, the most important are our feelings, not a ready description.

In this short book, I mainly present my own observations and experiences with cards. This is not a ready manual for reading Tarot cards regarding sexual life, but I believe that it will be helpful for many people, especially for beginners who are just starting their adventure with Tarot cards.

Major Arcana

The Fool

Sex

The Fool very often describes a lover with little experience and even a virgin (or losing one's virginity). A new lover who takes you to new levels of sexuality. An exciting and unpredictable lover with which we discover new sexual positions. Willingness to experiment, using sex toys, new sexual experiences.
It also shows someone who prefers unplanned and spontaneous sex, who likes to try new and unusual sexual positions, but the chances of a permanent relationship with him are slim.
The Fool also predicts sex with a stranger, casual sex adventure, one night stand, unprotected sex.
It also shows a penchant for younger partners.

In combination with the Devil card may indicate pedophilia.
In combination with the Two of Wands - homosexual tendencies.

Love

Upright:
flirt, romance, getting pregnant, birth of a child, initiative, date invitation, message, spontaneity, deep fascination, spending time together, common interests, strong feelings but it`s not a love yet, new admirer, new relationship, love at first sight

Reverse:
immature and irresponsible partner, infantile relationship, pretending feelings, lack of common interests, younger partner, betrayal, lack of spontaneity, no contact, stagnation, partner who does not love but only plays with us

The Magician

Sex

This card shows us a partner who excites words and a long foreplay.
He likes sensitive or dirty words whispered into ear.
He also likes to be adored, touched and stroked and likes to use sex gadgets, aphrodisiacs.
The Magician tells us about the long foreplay, about building tension through words, often dirty words. It can mean hot text messages from a partner, even a phone sex.
Sex on the table, desk, in different places, but not in bed.

In combination with 8 of Wands confirms the exchange of dirty messages between partners, sexting and sometimes phone sex or by other types of communicators.
In combination with The Empress - sending to each other hot or naked pictures.

Love

Upright:
perfect agreement between partners, open communication of your needs, messages, long conversations, harmony, fidelity, partner who cares about us, initiative, new stage in a relationship, new circumstances

Reverse:
difficulties and misunderstandings between partners, lack of honesty, competition between partners, trivial relationship, lies, mutual deception, relationship based on sex, infidelity, looking for sexual adventures, no initiative

The High Priestess

Sex

The High Priestess shows us a shy partner who is ashamed of his body, who is ashamed to come out with the initiative.
He has a lot of knowledge about sex, however, he is afraid to initiate sex and experiment, he has complexes. Only the right partner can awake passion in him and free the beast. If you pull this card out, you have to take the initiative.
The partner shown in this card rather connects sex with feelings, it is very important to him, expects spirituality in sex, the unity of souls.
The High Priestess often shows a partner who treats sex as a marital duty, of coercion, but it should be confirmed by other cards; like The Justice.
Sex rather polite, calm, under the duvet in the dark, missionary position.

In combination with The Hermit – renunciation of sex.
In combination with The Tower- sex from coercion, rape.

Love

Upright:
warm partner but secretive, distanced partner, very sensitive person who is easy to hurt, partner for whom the family is the most important, mutual respect and trust, deep and sincere feelings, love, harmony, fidelity, delicacy

Reverse:
betrayal, hiding something, secrets, avoiding conversations with a partner, misunderstandings, destructive influence of the mother's partner on the relationship, egoism, no action, lack of love, stagnation, shyness, no contact, fears, dark secrets, sensitiveness

The Empress

Sex

The Empress shows us a partner with high sexual needs about whom he is not ashamed to speak, he likes his body and is not ashamed to show it.
If we ask about a man, it shows us a type of visual. If we ask about a woman, it shows us beautiful woman who likes to show her advantages in public.
This card speaks about partner who likes sex and often has several lovers, he may be married.

Sex that is comfortable, passionate, joyful, partner focused.
Sex during which the partner's body is well-seen, definitely not under the quilt and not in the dark.
Sex which is planned with details, often to conceive a child.
The Empress may mean pregnancy, but should be confirmed by other cards, like: Ace of Wands, The Star or The Moon.

Love

Upright:
stable relationship, future wife, joint plans, buying a house, material security, happiness unconditional love, messages, fidelity, joy invitation, pregnancy, realization of plans, big love, dream partner, warm and loving woman, future mother of your children

Reverse:
betrayal, partner has a lover, quarrels, man who is afraid of women and does not trust them, manipulating the partner, lack of love, domination, unwillingness to get involved in a relationship, emotional immaturity, unwillingness to get pregnant, sexual blockage

The Emperor

Sex

The Emperor speaks about a partner who is very experienced in sex matters which he will certainly want to prove.

He is excited by domination and strength, in sex he is determined, he likes to lead.

In combination with The Tower, The Devil or 5 of Swords may show a taste for sadomasochism.

Sex with an older partner, often with an employer or with someone who has the power and money. Sexuality to gain promotion.

Traditional, classic sex often with a permanent partner, usually, where the man dominates and sets the rules, where the man is active.

If we ask about our spouse, the Emperor shows us a very routine sex.

In gay relationships, the card shows us which partner is active.

Love

Upright:
permanent partner, future husband, good husband and father, new interesting partner, stable relationship, true love, fidelity, partner you can rely on, if you're single, you'll meet the right partner very soon, future father of your children, initiative, news

Reverse:
fight for domination in a relationship, lover, woman who is afraid of men, lack of feelings, looking for a lover, unwillingness to engage in a long-term relationship, unwillingness to have children, partner who has a bad influence on you, tyranny, aggression, callousness, obstinacy

The Hierophant

Sex

The Hierophant describes a partner who likes clear rules of the game, a partner who will tell you what he expects. He must be sure that you really want it, otherwise he will not come out with the initiative. Do not expect spontaneity, it's not the type of spontaneous lover.

He likes to watch other people having sex, porn movies, magazines for adults, oral sex, he is often lazy in bedroom.

This card also means soulful and tantric sex, with confessions of eternal love. Sex with this one unique person, proposal of marriage (especially in combination with 4 of Wand or Ten of Cups).

The Hierophant sometimes shows us sex with a religious person. Religious advice on love and sexual teaching an inexperienced partner.

Love

Upright:
consistent and happy marriage, older partner, lasting feelings, faithfulness and loyalty,   strong emotional bond between the partners, wedding, engagement, religious partner

Reverse:
betrayal, crisis in relationship, marital therapy, lack of tolerance, misunderstandings, partner who is married and hides it, manipulation, domestic tyrant, relationship for strengthening the social position

The Lovers

Sex

The Lovers card describes us a very tender and delicate lover, who is a great romantic.

Shows us a lovers who are very similar in outlook, interests, who are neighbors.

Sex described in The Lovers is connected with strong feelings, with desire, very romantic with candles or by the glow of stars, very often somewhere in the nature. Sex such as in romantic movies with a lot of tenderness, hugging each other, stroking.

Often sex for agreement after quarrel, especially in combination with 5 of Wands.

In combination with The Moon or 2 of Wands, or 2 of Pentacles means hesitation in matters of sex and in choosing the right partner.

In combination with The Hangman or The Temperance describes routine sex, like in an old marriage.

Love

Upright:
Happiness, sincere and deep love, trust, fidelity, perfect understanding, mutual care, common goals, new relationship, new friendship, desire, passion, hesitation, choice between two people, harmony, date invitation, starting a family

Reverse:
destructive relationship, end of love, ending the relationship, manipulating the partner, fear of love, morbid jealousy, lack of trust, lack of love, infidelity, complexes, laziness, lack of contact, separation, sexual coldness, impotence, lies, inability to make a decision

The Chariot

Sex

The Chariot shows us fast sex, in a hurry and in unusual places, often risky and exciting.

It often takes place in means of locomotion, in the car, in the train, in the bus or on a plane.

Crazy, wild and often in a random place and where the lovers are partially dressed and uncomfortable place somewhere where other people can see us.

The Chariot describes a partner who likes fast and dangerous sex, opportunity to be seen by others excites him. He likes risk and experiments, he also likes to control partner, sometimes even tie him up.

In combination with The Emperor firm control and domination over the partner.

In combination with 5 of Wands – group sex.

Love

Upright:

Good news, joint trip, meeting a new partner during the trip, strong and dynamic feelings, fidelity, e-mail, sms from beloved person, invitation, initiative, success, victory, spending time together

Reverse:

Temporary separation, stagnation in a relationship, bad news from a loved one or about him/her, competition in a relationship, jealousy of a partner's success, no support, love gradually turns into hatred, misunderstandings, different plans, domination, vulgarity, cancellation of joint plans, obstacles, brutality

The Strength

Sex

The Strength describes a partner who is passionate and always eager for love frolics, has a huge desire for sex and extensive experience and skills. He likes sex and is eager to experiment in this field. He also often watches porn movies and has a taste for sadomasochism (especially in combination with The Devil, The Tower or 5 of Swords).

This card shows us a very passionate sex, uncontrolled and spontaneous with the positions in which the woman dominates; rider, straddle, reverse cowgirl, chair etc.

Often means passion that is difficult to control, it also means the fertile days of a woman (especially in combination with The Empress).

Love

Upright:
strong emotional ties, desire, true love, lasting relationship, mutual support, fidelity, initiative, message, courage, willingness to act

Reverse:
emotional emptiness, lack of desire, aggression, physical violence, brutal partner, quarrels, victim of an addiction, gambler, manipulation, impulsiveness, jealousy destroying the relationship, irresponsibility, betrayal, lack of love

The Hermit

Sex

The Hermit usually shows sexual abstinence, leading a life of celibacy, abstinence so do not count on passionate night with him. He lives in celibacy and does not even think about sex, he has more important things in his mind.

If you can persuade him to have sex it will be sex in a hidden place or with the lights off.

Sometimes this card speaks about feeling alone or a secret passion or obsession for someone.

The Hermit also shows us a masturbation.

In combination with 5 of Pentacles means begging our partner for sex.

In combination with 5 of Cups - unwillingness to have sex because of disappointment.

In combination with 10 of Wands - unwillingness to have sex because of fatigue.

In combination with The Death – asexuality or impotence.

Love

Upright:
older partner, marriage of convenience, despite misunderstandings, there will be no divorce, a relationship that gives you a sense of security, mutual respect, lack of passion, stagnation

Reverse:
being with someone because of fear of loneliness, relationship with habit and because of duties, emotional and sexual frigidity, no contact, isolation, the feeling of being misunderstood by the partner, disappointment, rejection, egoism

The Wheel of Fortune

Sex

The Wheel of Fortune shows us unexpected and spontaneous sex, be prepared for an intense experience. Frequent change of sex positions, often also partners, good fun, experimenting.
Sometimes sex for political or financial gain (especially in combination with Page of Pentacles or Knight of Pentacles).
Partner who will certainly initiate sex, he likes when a lot happens, he likes to change partners and enjoys group sex. He likes partners who know what they want, have experience and are willing to experiment.

Love

Upright:
karmic relationship, destiny, love for good and for bad, fidelity, lasting marriage, revival of feelings, unexpected change for the better, partner's return, new friendships, flirt, happiness, new beginning

Reverse:
quarrels and misunderstandings, disloyalty, lack of love, cheating partner, sudden negative changes, crisis in relationship, bad luck, helplessness, resistance to changes

The Justice

Sex

The Justice shows us sex without much emotion and feelings, fast and only as a need of releasing the sexual tension. It`s an act where partner doesn`t count, the most important thing is to achieve sexual satisfaction for oneself.

In a question about permanent partner speaks about very predictable sex without passion and spontaneity, very often planned and thought out. Responsible and certainly careful with protection against pregnancy.

If we ask about our permanent partner it means sex for consent after the quarrel or as part of the reward for something.

It can also show a sex with a lawyer, judge, older partner. The legal aspects of sexuality.

The Justice describes a partner who is afraid of the consequences which carries the sexual act (pregnancy, diseases, commitment to a permanent relationship or he doubts his skills). It blocks him and he is careful with taking initiative.

In combination with The Devil – illegal sex (too young partner or a rape).

Love

Upright:
stable relationship, lasting feeling, fidelity, similar characters, joint decisions about the relationship, harmony, stabilization, confidence, honesty, loyalty, peaceful and lasting relationship but without passion, friendship between partners

Reverse:
Quarrels even physical violence in relationship, mutual blame, lack of understanding, end of love, lack of positive feelings, betrayal, divorce, separation, emotional coldness, marriage of convenience

The Hanged Man

Sex

Erection problems, impotence, fear of sexual approximation, reduced libido, unwillingness to have sex. However, if there will be a sexual act between the partners then it will be strange and unusual sex.
Preferences for binding partner, for using handcuffs etc.
Partner who likes slow sex and is lazy in bedroom.

In combination with The Wheel of Fortune – a partner who needs strong stimuli to be in the mood for sex (to have an erection).
In combination with 8 of Swords – suffering in silence in an abusive relationship.
In combination with Ace of Swords – abortion .

Love

Upright:
mutual understanding, perfect complementation of partners, common interests, fidelity, stagnation in a relationship, no action, refraining from making a decision, no contact, lack of initiative, delays, obstacles, cancellation of plans

Reverse:
Discouragement, lack of trust, avoidance of liability, blaming others, jealousy, betrayal, obstacles, addiction to alcohol and drugs, toxic relationship, emotional blackmail, a person unable to love, lack of love

The Death

Sex

Unfortunately, we can`t say much about this card because it means almost no sex and interest in this topic. It shows us a sexual blocks. In combination with The Hermit – asexuality or impotence. In combination with The Devil – necrophilia.

He is not interested in sex with you, mainly because of some sexual blocks or erection problems.

Love

Upright:
Big changes, end of one stage and the beginning of a new one, new possibilities, change of feelings, painful break-up, divorce, new partner, often positive changes in the relationship - depends on the rest of the cards

Reverse:
negative changes in the relationship, fear of changes, love dies, infidelity, toxic relationship, accident, stagnation, serious illness of beloved person, suicidal thoughts, sadness, divorce

The Temperance

Sex

Normal, traditional sex without strange positions and experiments, missionary position.
The Temperance also shows us a lot of caresses and kissing, but no sex.
If there is a sex between partners then it's gentle and harmonious, but without deeper feelings.
Similar sexual preferences of partners, good temperament matching.

Your partner likes calm and gentle sex without a hurry, it is very important for him to match the temperaments and preferences between the partners.

Love

Upright:
Balanced and harmonious relationship, reasonable partner, perfectly matched partners, silent admirer, acceptance, stabilization, love, peace, patience

Reverse:
Intolerance, holding appearances, no acceptance, hesitation, problem with making a decision, capricious partner, emotional swing, lack of balance, lack of positive feelings, intrusive admirer, infidelity

The Devil

Sex

Brutal, licentious sex, toxic, dirty and full of deviations, without feelings, it's all about satisfying physical needs. Sex under the influence of stimulants: drugs, alcohol.
Sex in unusual positions, inventive techniques, gadgets.

In combination with The Tower – violence, body injury.
In combination with The Hermit - total lack of sex, but only obsession with him.
In combination with 9 of Pentacles - sex with prostitutes.
In combination with positive cards - very passionate and perverse sex.
In combination with 5 of Wands - beating a partner during love act and getting pleasure from it.
In combination with 3 of Swords - regular and numerous betrayals.
In combination with 5 of Swords - morbid jealousy and obsession with a partner.

Partner with a tendency to deviation, exhibitionism, sex addict.

Love

Upright:
strong desire, perfect sexual fit of partners, relationship based on having fun without deeper emotions, being used by a partner, dependence on a partner, success in the opposite sex, love affair, manipulation, one night stand

Reverse:
fear of sex, obsessive jealousy, sexual violence in a relationship, rape, sex for material benefits, perversions, betrayal, molestation, toxic relationship

The Tower

Sex

Rapid and simple sex, which quickly gives satisfaction and relaxation. Discovering shocking aspects of a partner's sexuality. Sex with someone in the military.

In combination with 8 of Swords or The Hangman - erection problems or a woman who has difficulty with reaching an orgasm.
In combination with Ace of Wands or 8 of Wands - quick ejaculation
In combination with such cards as The Star, The Sun or 4 of Wands - satisfying orgasm.
In combination with Ace of Swords- losing virginity, sometimes painful.

Partner who doesn't like to wait, likes quick sex, often he is not interested in the partner's satisfaction, but in his own pleasure.

Love

Upright:
possible parting or divorce (depends on the rest of the cards), quarrels that lead to separation, crisis in relationship, cooling down feelings

Reverse:
disregarding the partner, lack of feelings, divorce, painful break-up, numerous betrayals and affairs, sudden painful changes, impossibility to save a relationship, there is no chance for a partner to return, definitive end of the relationship

The Star

Sex

The Star describes us beautiful sex, full of feelings. Romantic and unhurried which is connected with the feeling of true love. The act is subtle, delicate and very satisfying.
Delicate partner, romantic type who likes calm and gentle sex, climatic with feelings of love. He likes to make love in the nature, in the forest, on the meadow, on the beach etc. He likes to admire partner`s body, and also enjoys having sex in the bathroom in the shower.
In combination with The Empress can show a pregnancy, the same with Ace of Wands.
The Star sometimes talks about homosexual acts, but rather between two women than two men (especially when in combination with Queens or with The Moon).

Love

Upright:
deep feelings, true love, unselfish love, long-term relationship, trust, happiness, happy future, common plans, fidelity, shared passions, pregnancy, caring partner

Reverse:
disappointment, being abandoned by a partner, fear of showing affection, distance between partners, lack of loyalty and trust, lack of love, infidelity, lack of hope, unrequited love, bad luck

The Moon

Sex

The Moon describes a partner who does not know what he wants or hiding something, he often has a lover or he is constantly entangled in some kind of love affairs.

He likes love triangles, especially when we have a combination with such cards as 3 of Cups or 3 of Wands. He likes to fantasize, but he lacks the courage to realize these fantasies. He is hesitant and it is difficult to count on the initiative on his part. He prefers women who are really curvy.

Long foreplay, sometimes harmless deviations and fetishes. Desire to fulfill fantasies, but however, often there is no courage to do it. As it is a card of hesitation, indecision and secrets, it is worth looking at the cards surrounding it, to determine more, to discover what fantasies our partner has or what secrets he`s hiding.

Love

Upright:
date invitation, romantic dinner, hiding secrets from a partner, insincerity, affair, fascination but lack of love, fantasies, illusions, a sense of loneliness in a relationship

Reverse:
betrayal, unfavorable mother-in-law, boredom with a relationship, escape into the world of illusion, wrong partner rating, perfidious lies, no contact initiative, lack of love

The Sun

Sex

The Sun describes delicate, successful and satisfying sex often in the form of play in bright light, with a lot of love, petting and stroking. Stable sexual relationship, fidelity.
All positions from the back.
Sometimes The Sun speaks about sex with a rich or famous person for fame or money (especially in combination with Page of Pentacles).

The Sun is a card which describes very affectionate lover with an extensive experience, he will take care of the partner's pleasure for sure, but he does not like to use protections which limit his pleasure, like condoms. Sometimes he likes older partners.

Love

Upright:
happy period in a relationship, reciprocated love, stable relationship, possible pregnancy, success, nice surprise, fidelity, harmony

Reverse:
disappointment, betrayal, breakup of the relationship, destructive influence of the past on the relationship, being in a relationship for the good of the family, lack of hope and love

The Judgement

Sex

The Judgment describes unexpected and sudden sex but with the satisfaction of both partners. Very sensual with music, often in water or somewhere near it or just in the morning after waking up.

Partner which this card describes is a sensual lover that stimulates all senses and arouses fantasies. He likes to have control, but you can expect an orgasm with him, he really cares about the pleasure of his partner.

Love

Upright:
favorable changes in the relationship, emotional transformation, overcoming obstacles, partner's return, new stage in life, renewal of contact, coming to terms with someone, fidelity, stable feelings, forgiving partner

Reverse:
passivity and fears, inability to forgive, emotional coldness, inaccessibility, relationship that has no chance to survive, the family does not accept a partner, infidelity, stable feelings

The World

Sex

The World shows us a long and very successful sex, the one that unites lovers. Trying new, exotic sexual positions, something we have not tried yet.

Partner which this card describes is open to new experiences, curious and willing to experiment with you.
The World can mean a partner from another country or with another religious denomination.
Often it's just sex on vacation, during some trip (especially in combination with The Chariot).

Love

Upright:
partner met during the trip, foreigner, love, support, lack of complexes, full of happiness, romantic love, fidelity, contact initiative, messages, stabilization, birth of a child

Reverse:
emotional coldness, fear of involvement, incoherence of characters, misunderstanding in a relationship, lack of positive feelings, stagnation, no initiative, disappointment

Minor Arcana -Wands

Ace of Wands

Sex

Your partner is very passionate lover, he loves to seduce, definitely takes the initiative when he is interested. He does not wonder, he works fast and he quickly excites himself, he is always and everywhere ready for sex. He uses every opportunity he gets, unfortunately just as he quickly begins just as quickly ends.

Ace of Wands describes sudden and rapid sex, but very joyful. Great desire, difficult to control.
Definitely in untypical places, where we want at the moment and the opportunity will come - here and now. Standing positions, or by the wall.
In combination with The Chariot can show sex in the car, before you`ll get to the place of the date.
Unfortunately, it usually means a quick sex without a night spent together and common future.

Love

Upright:
new relationship, pregnancy, the birth of a child, sexual initiation, mutual attraction between partners, desire, passionate period in relationship, creation, invention, new possibilities, motivation, courage, fertility.

Reverse:
infertility, miscarriage, sexual problems, conflicts, sexual abuse, moving away from the partner, expiration of feelings, coolness in relationship, fall, stagnation, restrictions, fear of changes.

Two of Wands

Sex

Two of Wands describes a calm, composed lover which should not be pressed, do not count on sex on the first date, your partner is not that type of man. You have to take the initiative, but do it gently and carefully, slowly and without pressure. Partner who is waiting for the right lover, he likes to be cuddled.

What sex describes this card?
With a partner who would like to, but he is afraid
Very delicate sex, with lots of stroking, touching and hugging, with hesitation: maybe here or maybe there, maybe this position or maybe another one.
Two of Wands in combination with some cards may show homosexual love:
In combination with Ace of Wands – gay love.
In combination with Ace of Cups – lesbian love.

Love

Upright:
strengthening the relationship, date, sex, fascination, sexual attraction, making a choice, communication, making plans, first step, reflecting on actions

Reverse:
unpleasant surprise, misunderstandings, conflicts, isolation, silence, fear of closeness, fear, physical suffering, restlessness, hesitation, no agreement

Three of Wands

Sex

Three of Wands describes intense and hot sex in an unusual place, often points to sex in the love triangle or the interest of one of the partners in this topic.
Oral sex, 69 position, anal sex, a lot of experimenting, often also sex under the tent, during delegations, on holidays.

Partner who likes to flirt and often does it with different people, he likes oral sex and has fantasies about sex with two partners at once. He likes to experiment, unfortunately, do not count on his fidelity.

In combination with The Wheel of Fortune - definitely indicates group sex.
In combination with 6 of Pentacles- partners exchange, swingers.
In combination with The Devil - addiction to sex.

Love

Upright:
new social contacts, short trip with a partner, greater intimacy, increased interest, commitment to the relationship, making plans, nice time together, building a house, realization of hopes, wealth, power, patience, partnership

Reverse:
competition with a partner, betrayal, conceit, arrogance, rejecting help, resistance to closeness, influence of a third party on the relationship, unwillingness to engage, deception, mistakes, isolation, difficulties in realization

Four of Wands

Sex

Four of Wands describes fast and intense sex, usually sex from the back, doggy style. Definitely not in bed and not gently. A relationship based on sex. This card shows sex in a closed space, at home, in some building very often with some erotic costumes or with erotic lingerie. with a huge physical attraction.

This card speaks about a partner who likes to admire a person with which he has sex.
He likes a lot erotic lingerie, all those laces and garters. He adores to seduce and tempt a partner, he loves to be admired and complimented. He also appreciates his partner and will not save compliments. He likes to flirt a lot.

In combination with cards on which water is shown, may show a sex in front of the mirror and admiring the act in it.

Love

Upright:
wedding, family party, happiness in the company of relatives, nice atmosphere between partners, stable relationship, harmony, peace, joy, blessings, family time

Reverse:
problems with a house, destruction of a harmony in relationship, misunderstandings, arguments, affair, frivolous relationship, lack of harmony, home conflicts, unreliable relationship

Five of Wands

Sex

Very spicy sex where both partners are very horny and passionate.
Quite often, sex that borders on violence, especially in combination
with such cards as The Tower, The Devil or 5 of Swords.
In combination with The Wheel of Fortune or 3 of Wands – group
sex with a quick change of partners, sometimes with the arguments
and fights for partners, aggressive group sex.
In combination with Ace of Cups – sex with woman during
menstruation.
In combination with The Tower or The Devil – with a person who
enjoys sex with violence, sadomasochism.
In combination with positive cards it simply means wild and
passionate sex quite often with a lot of moans and screams.
In combination with The Hangman or 8 of Swords - sex with
handcuffs, with tying a partner.

Five of Wands speaks about a partner who enjoys spicy sex, who
does not hesitate and takes what he wants , sometimes he is
aggressive.
In combination with The Emperor – a partner who dominates and
hates opposition.

Love

Upright:
competition, quarrels, fight for domination in a relationship,
competition for favors, searching for a new object of feelings, action,
lawsuit

Reverse:
a violent argument, different plans regarding the relationship,
weariness, impatience with partner and relatives, struggle, intrigue,
difficulties, open conflict

Six of Wands

Sex

Six of Wands speaks about a partner who is very confident, convinced of his skills and knowledge of various sexual positions. He likes to feel important, loves to listen to praises and compliments. He may want to dominate you, he also often gets into romance, even with the wife of his friend.
In the combination with The Moon - fast sexual act in hiding, so that no one would see.

Sex in the rider position, intense, passionate and satisfying for both partners.
One of the partners will be definitely dominate over the other and expect praise for his exploits.
Which one? If there will be combination with The Emperor or Kings – a man.
With The Empress or Queens- a woman.

Love

Upright:
good news, return of a former partner, many admirers, engagement, successful relationship, harmony, confession of feelings, happiness in love, victory, success, triumph, help from friends

Reverse:
double-faced friend or lover, delay, indecision, doubts, restrictions, breaking the engagement, delays, ingratitude, narcissism, false optimism, vaunt

Seven of Wands

Sex

This card shows us sex full of violence, of coercion, nervous, fast, in silence, with huge dominance one of the partners. Sexual act where one of the partners does not want that, he is forced.
In combination with The Devil, The Tower or 5 of Wands – rape (these cards intensify violence),
In combination with 9 of Swords – fear that the partner will hurt us or that someone will cover us.

Seven of Wands describes a partner who does not want to hear a refusal, who will force you to do what he wants, he can even go to manipulation to get what he wants and even to violence. He is not interested in giving pleasure to the other person.
Good when the accompanying cards are positive then, they will definitely ease the aggression and violence contained in 7 of Wands.
In combination with 6 of Pentacles - a sponsor who pays for sex and requires aggressive sex.

Love

Upright:
joint implementation of plans, overcoming obstacles, firm actions, conversations with a partner that brings good changes, victory, confrontation

Reverse:
an awkward situation, tense atmosphere between partners, defensive attitude, suspiciousness towards the partner, unwanted meeting, uncertainty, rumors, confusion, anxiety, ignorance, pretense, embarrassment

Eight of Wands

Sex

Eight of Wands describes very rapid and spontaneous sexual act, usually without a long foreplay.

This card speaks about joy at seeing you, your partner has an accelerated heartbeat, adrenaline and a great desire awakens in him. He is able to do anything to get you, he acts fast, usually before you moan the whole act will end.

This card often shows one night stand or random sex, in unusual places for example in the toilet.

Sometimes points to erotic conversations, flirt or phone sex.

The partner shown in this card is limbed and physically fit, he likes fast and disobliging sex. He is always ready to make love, but he also ends quickly. Do not count on a long and romantic night with him.

Love

Upright:
new love, intense and passionate relationship, random meeting, affair, infatuation, messages, sexual attraction, fast evolving relationship, movement, new options, new ideas, journey

Reverse:
misunderstandings, lack of feelings, betrayal, no chemistry between partners, lack of love, impatience, passivity, delay, stagnation, jealousy, some things cannot be hurried

Nine of Wands

Sex

Do not count on the initiative from your partner, if you want sex you`ll have to act.
This card hardly shows that there will be sex, rather tells us about bad sexual experiences for example about harassment. There is a huge dislike for sex in it. If there is sex, often it is sex with guilt and fear, sometimes with a great fear of unwanted pregnancy.
Sex next to the door, by the walls or on something hard (table, floor etc.).

Nine of Wands describes a partner who is very careful in matters of sex. He was hurt, somebody broke his heart and is now afraid to trust. He hides his feelings from fear, he isolates himself, but he covets you in secret. Sometimes he is just very shy and scared to do anything to get you.

In combination with 8 of Swords - blockage due to complexes.
In combination with 9 of Swords - fears of unwanted pregnancy or illness.
In combination with 7 of Wands- blockage due to sexual abuse in the past.
In combination with 3 of Swords- blockage due to broken heart.
In combination with 5 of Cups - because of disappointment in sex.

Love

Upright:
lack of trust, inability to forgive, sensitiveness, separation, unwillingness to engage more in a relationship, risking, resignation, displeasure

Reverse:
end of love, lies, betrayal, violence in relationship, unwillingness to meetings and conversations, obstacles, fear from being hurt

Ten of Wands

Sex

Ten of Wands describes a partner with high sexual needs, but having problems with satisfying them, usually because of stress and fatigue. He is overworked both physically and mentally. It is hard for him to cut himself off from problems and for this reason he is not in the mood for an erotic frolics.

In combination with The Hangman- erection problems, impotency . In combination with 2 of Swords - problems with expressing feelings, aversion to sex.
In combination with 5 of Wands - avoiding sex due to arguments between partners.
If you want sex you`ll have to act, you must take the initiative and you have to try very hard.

Upright:
emotional problems, difficulties in relationship, misunderstandings, relationship from a sense of duty, overwhelming with problems related to partner, need to rest

Reverse:
being used by a partner, being involved in someone`s problems (partner, kids, parents), jealousy, betrayal, toxic relationship, intrigues, loss, separation

Page of Wands

Sex

Random sex with a stranger, newly known partner. One night stand, or few meetings with the same partner but nothing obliging, a short relationship based on sex.
A lot of experimenting, trying new positions and toys, spicy and not monotonous sex.

Page describes a partner who does not like routine, but he loves freedom. He is not looking for a permanent relationship, he likes to change partners often, sometimes he meets several at once.
He does not like restrictions, he likes to break the rules. He is always willing to have sex, he is not picky when it comes to choosing a partner. Your lover likes to play and treats sex as entertainment, he is constantly looking for new incentives and new sexual experiences.

In combination with The Fool- an inexperienced lover who sleeps with everyone who is eager, he just wants to gain experience.

Love

Upright:
sincerity, truthfulness, nice surprises and meetings, passion but not love yet, looking for sexual adventures, message, unexpected meeting, contact, creativity, young person

Reverse:
delation, wrong information, disloyal partner, tactless behavior, stagnation, self-conceit, falsity, false feelings, bad news, naivety, instability, gossips, heartbreaker

Knight of Wands

Sex

This card means huge physical attraction, partner literally burns with lust, he is impatient and he wants you now and here. Great passion and great intentions, but do not count on a long night together. Sex will be fast and wild, does not matter in what position, just in here and now.
Sex described in this card is like a plane flying, a lot of noise, but before you see it, it's gone.
Sex in public places.

Knight describes a partner who is impudent and determined, focused on gaining a goal and does not accept a refusal. He excites very quickly, has many fantasies which he willingly fulfill. He loves sex and challenges associated with it.

In combination with 3 of Cups – he only cares about sleeping with as many partners as possible.

Love

Upright:
moving to a new home, good choice of the right partner, courage, pride, kindness, desire, passion, activity, action, initiative, meeting, message, date, strong and young lover, optimism

Reverse:
the urge to impress your partner or lover, ignoring the partner, arguments, misunderstandings, arrogance, egoism, vanity, discord, fear, jealous lover, lack of energy, frustration

Queen of Wands

Sex

A partner described in this card quickly takes the initiative, he likes to seduce in a feminine way, he likes long erotic games, and to build up the tension gradually. He has a lot of experience and also requires a lot from his partners. He is passionate and sexy, he loves to be adored and to be the center of attention, he also likes to dominate.

Queen of Wands shows sex in positions where a woman dominates and is active, with a long foreplay, with long seduction and temptation in sexy lingerie, but also very passionate with a satisfaction to both partners.

In combination with 5 of Wands - A woman who is a little too dominant, can even be slightly aggressive and scratch a partner.
In combination with 5 of Swords - A woman who likes BDSM, she likes to be tied, gagged.
In combination with The Devil – nymphomaniac.
In combination with Ace of Cups - A woman who quickly excites.
In combination with 9 of Cups – A woman who likes oral sex.

Love

Upright:
many social contacts and meetings, love adventure, sexual attraction, warm and noble woman, loving partner, magnetism, fertility, success, a woman who gets what she wants

Reverse:
infidelity, suspicious of betrayal, emotional blackmail, unsteadiness in feelings, brutality, aggression, lies, jealousy, revengeful woman, lack of self-confidence

King of Wands

Sex

King of Wands speaks about a partner who takes the initiative, he clearly shows interest in sex with you. He is very confident and it's hard to resist him, has extensive experience, he knows perfectly well where are the erogenous zones. He enjoys long foreplay, but the finale is usually fast. He is strong and durable so you can count on a long night, it's the card of a perfect partner. Let him take the initiative in bed and you will not regret it, will take care of you.

Sex in this card gives satisfaction to both partners, describes a long and passionate night with a long foreplay.

In combination with Two of Cups – sex connected with love, deep feelings.
In combination with 6 of Cups or with The Star – very romantic.
In combination with 10 of Wands - to lose your breath until you fall out of fatigue.

Love

Upright:
relationship with him is very passionate, honest, you can count on him, traditionalist, good father, reliable friend, strong and positive feelings, courage, risk taker, honor, generosity

Reverse:
despotism, criticizing the partner, empty promises, partner who dominates, difficult decisions, revengefulness, cold heart, duplicity, manipulation, ruthless, despotism, control, intolerance, violence

Minor Arcana - Swords

Ace of Swords

Sex

Ace of Swords speaks about sex without love, there is no feelings in that card. Technically correct, but without emotions and without much pleasure, do not count on closeness and feelings. In fact, there is a lot of conversation between partners in this card, it's a connection on an intellectual level, but complete lack of physical and emotional closeness, lack of satisfaction.

This card shows an experienced lover ,but not able to use this knowledge to please oneself and partner. In fact, he is not too much interested in you, you do not attract him too much. He can't show affection, he is cold.
This coolness of Ace of Swords can be mitigated by positive cards.

Love

Upright:
Similar intellectual level between partners, sincerity and honesty in relationship, forgetting about a painful past, release from toxic relationship and relatives, initiative, compromise, activity, justice, opportunity, determination, inspiration

Reverse:
Different opinions and plans, quarrels, gossips, words that hurt, manipulation, difference on intellectual level between partners, no compromise, sexual problems, brutality, obstacles, great loss

Two of Swords

Sex

This card shows the lack of sex, Two of Swords it is frigidity and aversion to a sexual act.
Sometimes it can show sex via the internet, webcams, erotic conversations, erotic photos, spicy talks, but rather the lack of real sex.

As in the case of Ace of Swords shows us a partner who is not too much interested in you, you do not attract him too much or he just has problems with showing emotions, he is afraid of intimacy.

In combination with 6 of Swords – lack of sex because of distances between partners, therefore, erotic conversations via the Internet appear.

Love

Upright:
Lack of trust, betrayal, jealousy, coldness, isolation, controlling emotions, uncertainty in relationship, pretending that the problem doesn`t exist, choice between two lovers, duality, blockage, indecision, being blind to something

Reverse:
Sexual coldness, emotional blockage, simulating feelings, moving away from partner, betrayal, lack of trust in relationship, painful decision, problem with making a decision, lack of tact, disloyalty, wrong choice

Three of Swords

Sex

Sex without love, in purpose to ventilate your bad emotions, sex for consolation, to forget about problems, for recovering from the bad day. Without paying attention to where, with whom and how. What counts is that sex was and it helped to relieve stress because, unfortunately, it did not give satisfaction. It brings emotional emptiness, the body has been satisfied, but the soul is not, something is missing here. Often shows sex that means physical pain, injury during sexual act or a painful loss of virginity.

Partner described in this card separates feelings from sex, he is not interested in serious and long term relationship. For him, sex is just an escape from problems and stress.

Love

Upright:
Disappointment, lies, love triangle, betrayal, being focused on bad emotions, words that hurt, separation, end of relationship, regret

Reverse:
Being focused on bad memories and events from past, incapability of characters, sudden misunderstandings, quarrels, feeling guilty, different plans, regret, sorrow

Four of Swords

Sex

This card shows the lack of sex and sexual abstinence, sleeping in separate beds.
In combination with 7 of Swords or The Moon - hidden venereal diseases
In combination with The Hangman – impotency
In combination with 9 of Wands – infertility

Partner described in this card is not interested in sex with you, you are indifferent to him, he does not feel physical attraction to you, or he just needs to rest, he is too tired with his problems and sex at this moment is beyond his interests. Check the other cards they will show you what is the reason for his indifference.

Love

Upright:
Temporary separation, distance to partner, emotional coldness, quiet days, rest from each other, isolation, lack of passion in relationship, loneliness

Reverse:
Marriage of convenience, being in a relationship because of fear of loneliness, definitive end of the relationship, lack of feelings, indifference, egoism, running away from problems

Five of Swords

Sex

Five of Swords shows us a partner who is egoist in matters of sex.
He cares only about his pleasure, and to satisfy his needs and
fantasies. He is also very jealous and it`s hard to him to control this
jealousy, he can be aggressive.
He likes brutal sex, sadomasochism, BDSM and gadgets like gags,
handcuffs etc.

Sex showed in this card is filled with strange fetishes like strangling
a partner, beating with a whip or role playing as a master and
servant.
There is not a lot of deep feelings and emotions in that sexual act,
there is only the need to satisfy strange preferences and fantasies
with the addition of a great and obsessive jealousy for a partner.

In combination with The Devil - morbid jealousy and obsession with
a partner.
In combination with 5 of Wands or 7 of Wands - sex with violence.

Love

Upright:
quarrels, end of relationship, fear from being abandoned, begging for
partner`s attention and feelings, misunderstandings, inability to share
money and feelings with partner, failure, cruelty, weakness, loss

Reverse:
Marriage of convenience, not noticing a partner`s needs, relationship
for money, shame, conflict, intrigue, manipulation, hidden enemies

Six of Swords

Sex

Sex showed in this card gives the beginning of the relationship with a new partner. There is a chance for long term and stable relationship, this is not a one night stand, it`s a beginning of a new stage in life. It is getting to know each other, partners are very curious of each other.
Often shows sex outside home, even in another city, the act is very calm, unhurried, careful.

Partner described in this card is very interested in you, he wants to know you better, he sees for future together. However, he is careful, he thinks and analyzes a lot and engages emotionally without hurry.

In combination with The World - partners who share the distance, one of the partners is in another city or country

Love

Upright:
Lack of contact, silence, hiding feelings, waiting for message or invitation, longing, physical separation, long distance relationship, movement but with obstacles, new places, journey by water

Reverse:
Toxic relationship, break-up, lack of willingness to forgive, manipulating the partner, isolation, emotional coldness, to avoid solving problems, delays

Seven of Swords

Sex

Seven of Swords speaks about a partner who is not honest with us, he lies very often and he is not faithful. He usually brags about his sexual skills, techniques and positions, he lies about how many partners he had.
It usually ends with bragging and nothing comes out of sex because he retreats at the last moment, probably because he is afraid that you will find out that he is a poor lover.

Sex in hiding, in secret, for example scared of parents sitting in the other room. In the dark, fast sexual act without much pleasure and emotions.

In combination with 3 of Cups - numerous betrayals

Love

Upright:
Sudden break-up, lack of contact, avoiding responsibility, unpaid promises, distance, unwillingness to show affection, lies, hiding something from partner, deception, gossips, secrets, spying on another, traitor

Reverse:
Malice, self-interest, empty promises, conspiracy, lack of perseverance, deceiver, lack of love, breaking the law, revenge, revengeful lover, hiding real feelings, temptation to cheat, taking a big risk

Eight of Swords

Sex

This card speaks about sexual blockade from your partners side, there is a blockade in him to new experiences, new positions and experiments. He also does not see the other person's efforts.
Sex in dark places, in small rooms or spaces in classic positions because partner is afraid of experiments.

Partner described in this card is not very interested in sex because of complexes, blockages and inhibitions. He is afraid of intimacy and avoids looking into a partners eyes, does not show feelings and is afraid of sex.

In combination with 7 of Wands - blockade because of sexual violence in the past
In combination with 9 of Wands- blockade because of complexes
In combination with 5 of Cups – he is afraid of disappointment

Love

Upright:
Loneliness, misunderstandings, fears, helplessness, lack of support from a partner, end of love, feeling of being in a cage, heavy childbirth, difficulties, disaffection, bondage, crisis, fear to move out, indecision

Reverse:
Inability of getting rid of a toxic relationship, crisis in relationship, lack of agreement, quarrels, lack of positive feelings, stillbirth, abortion, sorrow, depression, not noticing things

Nine of Swords

Sex

This card shows the lack of sex and no initiative from the partner.
It also speaks about thinking about problems in the sphere of sex,
frustration, nightmares, exaggerating problems.
If you want sex you need to take the initiative and be very patient.

Nine of Swords describes a partner who is afraid of sex, he is afraid
of disappointment, disease and exaggerates all these fears. He is not
ready for experiments, you`ll have to convince him, show him that
there is nothing to afraid.

In combination with 6 of Cups- very shy partner
In combination with 6 of Pentacles- fear of being abused

Love

Upright:
Unwillingness to enter into a relationship, feeling guilty, mourning,
hysteria, pessimism, desperation, doubts, shame, fear of losing a
partner, being with someone because of fear of loneliness, failure,
grief, nightmares, misery

Reverse:
Shyness, reticence, apathy, emotional violence, secrets, inability to
forgive, nightmares, fear for a loved one, a real threat to the
relationship

Ten of Swords

Sex

Very little chance that there will be sex, the partner does not want to have sex but if you will manage to convince him, then do not count on fire in the bedroom.
In combination with 7 of Wands- rape, forcing to have sex

Ten of Swords describes a partner who thinks he's bad in bed, a terrible lover and because of that he lacks the courage to take the initiative.

In combination with The Fool- he is not very experienced and hence his fears.

Love

Upright:
Bad news, disaster, lack of hope, tears, harm, break-up, betrayal, quarrels, separation, breaking the engagement, wedding cancellation, cancellation of common plans, obsession, desolation

Reverse:
Acceptance of breaking up with a partner, acceptance of difficult changes, and of toxic relationship, return of faith in better future, common decision of ending a relationship, breaking barriers

Page of Swords

Sex

Page of Swords describes a partner who has a lot of theoretical knowledge, but has little practical experience. He is open to experiments, unfortunately he can be very critical to his partner. He also likes using vulgar words during a sexual act. He often criticizes his partner and compares it to his ex.

Sex in this card is without much emotions, but there is a willingness to experiment, to test new techniques and positions. Often the foreplay is saturated with vulgar words.

In combination with 5 of Wands- very aggressive and vulgar sex
In combination with The Devil - addiction to vulgar sex

Love

Upright:
Unexpected message, date invitation, common interests, shyness, sms, e-mail, smart but little cold and impulsive partner, curiosity, innocence

Reverse:
Difficult partner, manipulator, unreliable, deceiver, a matrimonial cheater, gossipmonger, vulgarity, delays, being used by a partner, hesitation

Knight of Swords

Sex

This card describes a partner who is very brave and quickly takes the initiative and sometimes is violent. He does not think too much, he just acts. Unfortunately, it's a type of egoist which is only interested in satisfying his needs. He is not interested in a permanent relationship, he does not care about love, he is still looking for new sexual adventures.

Sex in Knight of Swords is fast, and not very satisfying for you, your partner cares only about his pleasure.

In combination with 6 of Wands - he will want to get you at all costs
In combination with 5 of Cups - lack of orgasm, disappointment
In combination with 9 of Pentacles – he will wish to pay you for satisfying his fantasies

Love

Upright:
A partner who likes intelligent conversations, active, clever, brave, honest, healing a broken heart, new social contacts, end of problems in relationship, messages, rapid movement

Reverse:
An attempt to get a goal at any cost (with force), talkativeness, confident, relationship of convenience, fiery partner, arrogance, coldness and inaccessibility, tyranny, impatience

Queen of Swords

Sex

This card speaks about a partner who has very high requirements with a strictly defined vision of the sex he likes. He will give you literally instructions what to do, how and where. He has a rationalistic approach to sex.

Sex describes in this card is without deeper emotions, without passion, it`s quite cold sexual act in classical positions, but with a lot of moans and screams. It also shows a lot of talking during sexual act, explaining to the partner what he should do.

In combination with Knight of Swords – an egoistic partner who will tell you what to do to satisfy him, in return you will get anything
In combination with The Emperor - partner dominates, directs you to please him
In combination with 9 of Cups – oral sex, but with pleasure for only one partner usually for a woman

Love

Upright:
Intelligent partner, independent, experienced, relationship without passion, common interests, diplomatic solving problems with a partner, widow

Reverse:
Prudery, mendacity, false morality, loss of beloved person, intrigue, vanity, conceit, wickedness, cunning, sexual coldness, emotional inaccessibility, relationship of convenience

King of Swords

Sex

King speaks about lack of emotions during sex, it`s very cold act where a man dominates and unfortunately he is an egoist.
This card often means oral sex where a woman is kneeling in front of a man.

Partner described in this card is the one who will take the initiative , but he is very dominant and cold. He does not show any feelings because he rarely feels anything. For him, sex does not have to be associated with emotions, it should just give him physical pleasure. He knows what he wants and is very experienced lover, but he uses that experience to his own pleasure.

Love

Upright:
Wise and mature partner, communication, messages, a partner who prefers relationship of convenience, cold partner who doesn`t like to show his emotions, strict parents, order, rationality, tactical

Reverse:
Not keeping promises, ruthlessness, cold calculation in relationship, naivety, egocentrism, difficult partner, relationship of convenience, criticism, self-interest, perversion, cruelty, bad intentions

Minor Arcana – Cups

Ace of Cups

Sex

Usually shows oral sex such where a man gives a pleasure to a woman. It is very delicate and tender sex, connected with deep feelings of people who have been attracted to each other for a long time. Passion, care, love, lots of kisses, it speaks through this card.

In combination with The Star - very romantic
In combination with The Strength – multiple orgasm

Ace of Cups describes a partner who has feelings for you, he is tender and delicate, he really cares about your pleasure. Quite often speaks about very shy partner, he likes you, but he's afraid to show it.
In combination with The Empress or Ace of Wands - pregnancy

Love

Upright:
New lover, beginning of new relationship, new, crazy and beautiful feelings, opening a heart, fertility, surprise, love against reason, happiness, opportunity, joy, abundance

Reverse:
Instability in love, unrequited feelings, rejected love, illusions, infertility, indifference, lack of trust, feeling lonely, false love, lack of willingness to act, feeling lost

Two of Cups

Sex

This card is dominated by feelings, it`s a sex of two people who are freshly in love with each other. Before anything happens between them, there is a lot of sexual subtexts in their conversations, looking to each other with lust in eyes.
Very affectionate and romantic sex with no rush, looking each other in the eyes during the act, in positions that allow you to observe the partner's reaction.

Two of Cups describes a partner who is in love with you and he will do everything to give you as much pleasure as he can. He will take care of a nice atmosphere, romantic dinner (candlelight dinner) etc. He wants to create an atmosphere that will connect not only the bodies, but your souls.

Love

Upright:
Harmonious relationship, first meetings, dates, getting to know each other, commitment to a relationship, attraction, balance, compromise,   if You already are in long term relationship – strong and deep feelings, forgiveness, second chances

Reverse:
Temporary separation, being bored with your partner, emotional instability, conflicts, quarrels, lack of compromise, lies, lack of love and passion, confusion, disunity

Three of Cups

Sex

Very joyful, cheerful sex with lots of laughter and jokes.
Often describes a sex treated as an entertainment, for fun, at a party
under the influence of alcohol or drugs (especially in combination
with The Devil).
Quite often also as an introduction to sex during different types of
games like strip poker etc.
Three of Cups is also a card of love triangles, so you can expect sex
with two partners.

This card describes a partner who likes to have fun, he is very
charming and likes to flirt and he is not a type of monogamist. He
likes sex in a triangles, often fantasizes about group sex.
Three of Cups speaks also about lesbian sex, especially in
combination with cards containing feminine energy.

Love

Upright:
Love affair, a lot of fun, conscious start of romance, common
interests, open relationship, spending time with each other, non-
binding meetings, positive outcome, success, luck

Reverse:
Falsity, abuse of trust, unwanted admirers, exaggerating someone`s
defects, lack of control over emotions, hiding feelings, relationship
just for fun, betrayal, love triangle, missing opportunities, fear of
taking action

Four of Cups

Sex

This card speaks about no desire for sex, exhaustion is shown here and discouragement about this topic. Often indicates depression, all kinds of reluctance to touch, no desire for erotic frolics.

In combination with 5 of Cups – disappointment with sex
In combination with 7 of Wands – being discouraged because of sexual abuse in the past
In combination with 10 of Wands - tiredness with problems

Four of Cups describes a partner who is not interested in sex, he is tired and focused on his problems. As a lover is not very good in these matters, he is lazy and not willing to experiment.
Sometimes this card means a small temperament, certainly smaller than yours and this is the source of problems in bedroom (especially in combination with 2 of Wands or Two of Pentacles)

Love

Upright:
Stagnation, inability to express feelings, passive attitude in relationship, cooling down feelings, boredom, not paying attention to the admirer, distraction, not seeing an opportunity, dissatisfaction

Reverse:
Indifference, someone who was very wronged and has a problem to trust and get involved in new relationship, searching for sexual adventure, being focused on past and partner`s mistakes, new ideas

Five of Cups

Sex

Shows us a sex which does not give satisfaction, it's disappointing, it is not what we expected.
Quite often it is related with disappointments and unpleasant memories related to past intimate experiences.
This is definitely an unsuccessful sex, often with a regular partner who disappoints us all the time, who does not care about us or he can`t fulfill our expectations. Sometimes it is sex on which we decide because of the feeling of guilty, willingness to compensate our mistakes (especially in combination with The Justice)

Five of Cups describes a partner who has prejudices and sex is not pleasant for him because of earlier experiences. It takes a lot of patience to change it, do not push and take initiative carefully.

Love

Upright:
Emotional lesson, difficult relationship, fear, loss, sorrow, end of relationship, lack of love, no contact, disappointment, regret

Reverse:
Toxic relationship, emotional dependence, marital crisis, avoiding to end of a difficult relationship, desperation, disappointment, lack of feelings, feeling lonely in relationship

Six of Cups

Sex

Six of Cups speaks about very delicate and tender sexual act. This card it is full of romanticism and warm feelings. Very often means a lot of caresses and kisses, but without sex. If there is a sexual act, it`s very subtle between two people who have feelings to each other. The partners are a little bit ashamed of themselves and are not inclined to crazy experiments.

This card describes a partner who is very gentle and great lover, he is often a bit shy and can`t believe his skills. Rather rarely comes out with initiative despite being interested to you. He likes subtle and gentle caresses with a large dose of kisses, gentle massage and long foreplay. He really cares about his partner`s pleasure, sex for him should be related with feelings.
In combination with The Strength - long and passionate sex with a large dose of deep feelings, with love.

Love

Upright:
Message, return of an old friend or lover, positive memories, back of an ex partner, idealizing a partner, desire to have children, new opportunities

Reverse:
Toxic emotions, anger, irritation, grief, conflicts, uncertainty, addiction to the family, destructive influence of parents on relationship, controlling parents, lack of responsibility, living to much in the past, avoiding confrontation with reality

Seven of Cups

Sex

Seven of Cups describes a partner who is addicted to sex, he often changes partners. He loves weird sexual positions, sex in front of cameras, recording his sexual feats, love triangles etc. For him there are no restrictions on these matters. He has a huge imagination, so you will not be bored with him.
He will definitely take the initiative and will want to implement all of his wildest fantasies with you.

This card speaks about intense sex without limits. Here is a huge desire which is difficult to satisfy.
Implementation of the wildest erotic fantasies with the use of many gadgets, continuous change of positions, implementation of bold ideas, often sex under the influence of alcohol or drugs.

In combination with The Wheel of Fortune – group sex
In combination with The Devil - sex addiction, depravity

Love

Upright:
Dreams without taking action, illusion, being uncertain about your feelings, hesitancy, deception, more than one choice, two potential partners, dreamer

Reverse:
Platonic love, false image of relationship and partner, illusions, unfulfilled promises, hesitation, flightiness, internal emotional conflict, waking up to action

Eight of Cups

Sex

The card speaks of boredom with the current partner, sex with him no longer enjoys. There is a desire to try something new, desire for betrayal, because we are not satisfied with our current sex life.
Sex in this card is monotonous, routine, it lacks fire and passion, in classic positions without any experiments.

In combination with 7 of Cups - fantasies about another partner during a sexual act
In combination with 3 of Cups – love triangle

This card describes a partner who will not come out with the initiative and his current sexual life does not satisfy him. He wants to try something new, but has no courage or he is simply lazy. He is a boring lover, always unhappy and he does nothing to change it.

In combination with 2 of Pentacles - he does not know what he really wants
In combination with 9 of Cups - he likes to satisfy himself (masturbation)

Love

Upright:
Emotional dilemmas, wondering if to stay in a relationship or leave, tiredness, emotional swing, moving on, rejection, travel, restart, changing direction

Reverse:
Expiration of feelings, broken ties, troubles in relationship related to money, lack of strength to leave toxic relationship, grief, sadness, being abandoned by lover, sudden break-up, fear of change and loss

Nine of Cups

Sex

Nine of Cups shows us a partner who likes oral sex, he also likes to entertain himself alone –masturbation, especially in combination with The Hermit or 8 of Cups. Partner who loves sex and is always willing to come out with the initiative, he will tempt and persuade you. It's a bit of a selfish card, so do not count on his commitment, he will expect you to fulfill all his desires and he will not care about your desires.
This card speaks about oral sex with a partner who is egoist and is focused on his own pleasure.
Sometimes this card shows a foreplay during which one of the lovers is masturbating himself in front of his partner, he does it to encourage his partner to common frolics.

In combination with 9 of Pentacles - sex for money, using the services of prostitutes
In combination with The Chariot - a quick oral sex somewhere in the car, train or bus

Love

Upright:
Pleasure, selfishness in relationship, he/she cares more about his/hers pleasure, granted wishes, abundance

Reverse:
Emotional blockage in relationship, demanding attitude towards partner, unjust judging of a partner, stubbornness, conservatism, false freedom, your wish will not be fulfilled

Ten of Cups

Sex

Classic sex at home, calm and quiet, often routine like in an old marriage. Despite the lack of madness and experiments in this sexual act, it's a lot of feelings here, commitment and taking care of a partner. Missionary position, often under the blanket and in the dark.

In combination with 4 of Cups or 8 of Cups- boredom with the present lover
In combination with 7 of Cups - fantasizing about the fact that we want a different sex
In combination with The Hierophant - marital sex
In combination with 2 of Cups - marital sex, but still with deep feelings of love

This card describes a partner who does not like to experiment, he prefers the positions he already knows, routine is his middle name. Do not expect crazy nights with him, but you can be sure that he will take care of your pleasure because he still cares about you.

Love

Upright:
True love, warm feelings, starting a family, fulfillment, wealth, security, safety, completion and success for all

Reverse:
Interferences of parents in a relationship, unfulfilled promises, lies, quarrels, disappointment, lack of independence, controlling family, lack of own will, manipulation, pressure, jealousy, touchiness, misplaced trust, false happiness

Page of Cups

Sex

Page of Cups shows us a very shy and bashful partner who is ashamed to show naked in front of his lover, sometimes he is also inexperienced. Rather, he will not come out with the initiative, he will not try to dominate ,but he will obediently follow his partner's instructions in bedroom. He is excited about watching other couples having sex. He is also very sensitive to any stimuli, touch, taste, smell, stimulating these senses is the key to success.

Sex in this card is full of coquetry, a bit shy and short during which delicate spanking may occur. Stimulating the partner's body with various things to wake his senses, touch, spanking, massage with the use of oils etc. Sometimes a striptease of one of the lovers.

In combination with 7 of Swords - watching others or watching porn
In combination with 6 of Swords - sex in hiding or in the dark

Love

Upright:
A friend you can always count on, shy admirer, warm but not deep feelings, message, news, enthusiasm, spontaneity, gentle friend, younger lover

Reverse:
Deep feelings for a person who is not worth of our love, lies, indiscretion, sacrificing yourself for an unworthy partner, unstable feelings, pretending to be a victim, disappointment in love, unrequited feelings, obstacles, ignoring emotions, seduction

Knight of Cups

Sex

This card describes a partner who is not the type of monogamist, often changes lovers, he has a tendency to many betrayals. Quite often he has many partners at one time. Despite these drawbacks, sex with him is a real land of pleasure, he knows how to satisfy his partner and sometimes he can be romantic when the need arises. He is delighted with the body of his lover, he compliments a lot.

Sex in this card is very passionate, in the right atmosphere, pleasant for both partners. Rather, without a long foreplay, but with experiments.

In combination with The Devil – he is a perverse lover
In combination with 9 of Cups – oral sex

Love

Upright:
Message, love at first sight, strong and romantic feelings but not permanent, proposition, seduction, warm feelings, date

Reverse:
Obsessions and perversions, revengefulness, hiding your desires from a partner, lack of scruples, insolence, emotional unavailability, fraud, chaos, duplicity, illusions

Queen of Cups

Sex

Sex combined with deep feelings, with love, where the man dominates and the woman obeys and tries to please the partner, her own pleasure is not so important to her. Positions from the back, where a man dominates.

In combination with negative cards, often means manipulating a partner on a principle of punishment; you did not throw away the rubbish, so do not count on sex.

A partner for whom sex without love does not exist and takes care of your lover's pleasure.
In combination with The Justice - sex as a marriage obligation
In combination with 7 of Wands - partner manipulation to get what you want

Love

Upright:
Strong and deep feelings, deep connection, caring partner, love, joy, pleasure, supportive partner

Reverse:
Illusions, narcissism, unfulfilled desires, pessimism, unrequited feelings, cowardice, changeable moods, perversion, blockages

King of Cups

Sex

Classic sex without bigger ecstasies, but connected to feelings, with engagement, usually in a missionary position. The surrounding cards will tell us more here, there is no crazy sex in this card.

King is a partner who is constant in feelings, he does not expect too much in sex, it's just supposed to be correct and with emotions. He settles what he gets and is happy. However, he has a high ego and can easily be offended, he hates criticism.
In the company of negative cards means a manipulator who cheats a partner to satisfy his needs (especially in combination with The Devil, The tower or 7 of Wands)

In combination with 6 of Wands – he expects compliments, praise his abilities and this will be the key to your pleasure.

Love

Upright:
Loving and protecting but sometimes jealous partner, family is for him most important, loving dad, he does not like to show affection, wise man, future husband

Reverse:
Scandal, disgrace, quarrels, difficult and discordant relationship, manipulation, falsity, feigned feelings, mental issues, powerful man but violent, injustice

Minor Arcana - Pentacles

Ace of Pentacles

Sex

Ace of Pentacles often shows us pregnancy, sex to conceive a child, planning a child in positions where the woman completely gives herself to the man. This is not a card full of crazy passion, it's simple, classic sex mainly to conceive a child.

This card describes a partner who does not treat sex as pleasure, for him it`s just a way to conceive a child. He is practical, do not count on romanticism or passion on his part. He is a good man, feelings are important to him, he takes care of his partner, also financially. Often, sex for him is simply a marital duty.

Love

Upright:
Emotional stability, sense of security, common future, planning a common future, initiative, engagement, wedding planning, common living, satisfaction, purchase of land or house, gift, surprise, date, fresh start, chance, success

Reverse:
Lack of stability and security, break of promise, jealousy, rapacity, marriage articles, separate bank account, miserliness, marriage of convenience, an attempt to buy love, materialism, lack of feelings between partners

Two of Pentacles

Sex

Two of Pentacles describes a partner who does not know what he wants, he is also not sure about his sexuality. Sometimes this card shows a bisexual person. He is hesitant and very changeable, therefore, he tests various techniques and sexual positions. He does not like sex in a hurry, but he likes group sex, he can be a swinger.

Sex in this card is without rush, partners test different sexual positions and they like to experiment. This is mainly due to their hesitation what they really like. There is no deeper feelings in this act, it is a typical relationship of friends with benefits.

In combination with The Wheel of Fortune – group sex
In combination with 8 of Cups - Swingers' adventures due to boredom in a relationship
In combination with 2 of Wands - homosexuality
In combination with The Fool or Page of Swords - a little experienced lover who wants to discover what he really likes

Love

Upright:
Common strengthening the material position in relationship, harmony, understanding in relationship, common plans, happy family, stabilization, new social contacts, making a choice, messages from far away, balance

Reverse:
Hypocrisy, hesitation, no compromise, dissidence, relationship without commitment, lack of emotions and passion in relationship, different plans for life, indecision, no choices left, no contact

Three of Pentacles

Sex

This one shows us very long and intense sex, it squeezes all the sweats out of the partners. Without feelings, often a purely physical approach to sex. The card shows that the partners are honing their skills with each other. They learn new positions and techniques together, they test positions requiring extraordinary efficiency and strength. Together they are looking for new experiences that will give the greatest pleasure.

This card describes a partner who is physically strong, he can make love for a long time and many times, a long and amazing night awaiting for you. He eagerly tests new techniques and positions because he wants to be the best lover and he is constantly looking for stronger and stronger pleasures.

In combination with The Wheel of Fortune- very often change of position
In combination with 5 of Wands - long and rough sex

Love

Upright:
Engagement, lasting and reliable relationship, material stabilization, partners who working together on a relationship, persistence, common plans, common pursuit of the goal, new options

Reverse:
Unwillingness to work on a relationship, escape from problems, workaholics, betrayal, someone else affects on the relationship, marital therapy, lost chances, obstacles

Four of Pentacles

Sex

This card describes a lover who has sex mainly to keep his partner with him. He does not like it too much, but he does not want to be alone. He is not interested in sophisticated techniques or positions, as long as this duty is already behind him.

Four of Pentacles speaks rather about a lack of sex, if it is then it's sex in home, monotonous where the partners do not give much.

In combination with 9 of Swords - fear of losing a partner
In combination with 8 of Wands - very fast sex, just to fulfill the duty
In combination with 7 of Wands - being forced to have sex by a partner by blackmail that he will leave us

Love

Upright:
emotional blockade, inability to show emotions, being with someone out of habit, self-serving, resistance to breaking up with partner because of fear of losing money, stopping the partner from leaving at any price, control, savings

Reverse:
controlling the partner, jealousy, need to receive proofs of love, passivity, lack of initiative, material miserliness, lack of emotions, self-interest, possessive, willingness to have partner at all costs

Five of Pentacles

Sex

This card has a total lack of sex, there will be no sex at all. The card also means begging for sex, especially accompanied by the The Hermit.

In the question of what kind of lover he is, describes a partner who does not care what sex will be, with whom and where. He is not a very good lover, he likes to be passive and allows to dominate his partner.

In combination with 8 of Cups - boredom with current partner
In combination with 3 of Cups - your partner does not want to sleep with you because he has someone else

Love

Upright:
quarrels, problems, lack of feelings and hope, misunderstandings, financial problems, not showing feelings, no contact, debts, indifference, passivity, expiration of feelings, sadness, loss

Reverse:
being in toxic relationship, fighting for money with your partner, loneliness, emotional poverty, mutual blaming, serious problems in relationship, time to rebuilding losses

Six of Pentacles

Sex

Very often shows sex for money, using the services of prostitutes especially accompanied by The Devil or 9 of Pentacles.
Sex with striptease as a foreplay.

Six of Pentacles describes a partner who connects sex with material benefits.
This card for me has double meaning, combined with positive cards means a partner who likes to give a lot of pleasure to his lover. In combination with negative cards, a partner who cares only for himself, an egoist.

In combination with King of Pentacles - rich sponsor

Love

Upright:
happy relationship where giving and taking are in balance, positive emotions, sense of security, mutual respect between partners, joy, generosity, honesty, buying a house, gift, attention

Reverse:
jealousy leading to material losses, duplicity, financial use of a partner, overprotection, financial dependence on the partner, material problems in family, bad debts

Seven of Pentacles

Sex

Routine sex in standard positions, quite monotonous and predictable. There is a lack of novelty and passion, it's the sex of old marriages. Also it often shows sex to conceive a child, intense efforts to get pregnant, waiting impatiently for the news of pregnancy. Sexual act is unhurried with a long foreplay.

Seven of Pentacles describes a partner who likes long foreplay, he likes when sexual arousal increases gradually. Despite the lack of deeper emotions here, he cares about his lovers pleasure, he is calm, a bit monotonous in bed. Do not count on the initiative on his part, rather he will expect it from you. He is a partner which will allow you to dominate.

Love

Upright:
patient waiting for appropriate partner, love which is slowly growing - where it`s born with time, lasting relationship, taking care of the relationship, temporary separation, slowing down the pace in a relationship, relationship development, serious intentions, planning

Reverse:
wrong moment to get involved in a relationship, impatience in a relationship, putting pressure on the partner, insist on getting married or engagement, platonic relationship, delays in the implementation of common plans, impatience, disappointment, obstacles

Eight of Pentacles

Sex

Eight of Pentacles speaks rather about a lack of sex, both partners want sex, but something blocks them, there are some obstacles, if there will be sex, it will be physically and emotionally draining for both lovers. This card speaks about sex at work, with the risk that someone will see us.

In combination with 9 of Pentacles or 6 of Pentacles - sex for profits, usually for promotion, some profit at work
This card describes a partner who has high sexual needs, usually in the category of quantity and not quality.

In combination with The Hangman – lack of sex because of the impotency
In combination with 10 of Wands - lack of sex because of problems and stress
In combination with 5 of Cups – lack of sex because of emotional or physical disappointment

Love

Upright:
marriage of convenience, practical approach to the relationship, working together on material stability, stagnation, lack of passion, jointly building a lasting relationship, writing a will, routine, hard work, dedication

Reverse:
miserliness, greed, emotional coldness, inability to express emotions, materialism, shame, apathy, feeling that what was the best in a relationship has already passed and will not come back, lack of ambition, intrigue

Nine of Pentacles

Sex

It is a card of prostitutes, describes a sex for money, for material benefits, sometimes for social benefits. Nine of Pentacles shows that the body is for sale.

Often shows sex in luxurious places, luxurious hotels, a very comfortable bed, places where there is glamour and where are rich people.

In combination with 6 of Pentacles – sponsorship

This card describes a partner who cares only about his pleasure and to satisfy his needs and fantasies. He also has no moral resistance for getting material benefits for sex. He likes to make love in glamour places, dazzling with wealth, it literally excites him. He loves luxury and this is the best aphrodisiac for him.

Love

Upright:
loneliness, living alone, single by choice, emotional distance, being together for convenience or money, independence, persistence

Reverse:
sense of loneliness, belief that love can be bought, paying for love, prostitution, sponsorship, using a partner, instability, lack of love, cancelled plans

Ten of Pentacles

Sex

Ten of Pentacles describes a partner who has big appetite for sex, he has huge sexual needs and fiery temperament. He cares about his lovers pleasure, he is trying to satisfy him with all strength. He also loves to use food in foreplay, good dinner with aphrodisiacs it's his favorite beginning of love frolics.

This card shows us sexual act which is very gentle with a lot of emotions. It is a sex where there is a food included in foreplay, it happens that partners play with food, licking food from the partner's body etc. Satisfactory for both partners.
As a place where sexual act happens , it`s usually during some trip to the countryside, quite often also a picnic on the meadow, in the park ended with sex.

In combination with pregnancy cards - scheduled sex to conceive a child

Love

Upright:
home buying planning, wedding, family meeting, rich partner, planning to start a family, material security, family tradition, safety, calmness, success for all, wealth

Reverse:
being together but being absorbed in your own affairs, lack of time for partner or kids, pathological family, quarrels, differences of opinion on the financial background, loss of a house, separation, divorce, brutality, sexual inhibition, emptiness

Page of Pentacles

Sex

Page of Pentacles describes a partner who is curious about new techniques and positions and is willing to experiment. He loves to educate himself, read about sex, watch erotic movies etc. He has a lot of theoretical knowledge and looks for opportunities to test it in practice. He loves to be praised and appreciated, he hates critics.

Sex showed in this card is long, where lovers are testing new techniques and positions. Together they polish their skills and are eager to win new ones. There is no a lot of feelings here, it is purely physical experience, without emotions.
Sex in places like school, training places, delegations, integration events.

In combination with The Magician - testing new toys for adults
In combination with The Wheel of Fortune- frequent change of positions

Love

Upright:
partner who calculates if the relationship pays off, good father, loyal partner however, feelings are not the most important thing for him in a relationship but money, reasonable, generous, good news, favorable circumstances, young lover, new ideas, learning

Reverse:
chaotic activities, miserliness, indifference, no romantic activities, greed, lack of feelings and passion, materialism, gambler, partner who will use us materially and will leave us

Knight of Pentacles

Sex

Knight of Pentacles as a sexual partner is very patient, but also very slow, in no hurry, he likes long foreplay. Sex for him should be combined with feelings, with love because he counts on a lasting relationship, he is looking for stability, he wants to start a family. He is well-endowed.

Sex showed in this card is technically correct, with no hurry, without much effort on both sides. Quite cautious, always with protection from fear of unplanned pregnancy.
Unfortunately also boring, monotonous without madness and the no will to experiment, in classic positions such as missionary position.

Love

Upright:
a loyal partner but emotionally unavailable, permanent and stable feelings, faithful, reliable traditionalist, a relationship for life, practical approach to the relationship, stable relationship but without passion, pragmatism

Reverse:
conservatism, putting pressure on the partner, materialism, quarrels, neglecting a partner, criticizing a partner, emotional coldness, lack of commitment, laziness, stagnation, carelessness

Queen of Pentacles

Sex

Partner described in this card has extraordinary seductive abilities. He loves to be surrounded by beauty and be beautiful, he takes care of himself. He diversifies his sex life by playing roles, in costumes or in sexy lingerie, he loves to be in a role of policeman/policewoman, nurse, doctor etc. He likes comfort, so no chance here for quick sex in the toilet or car, preferably in the bedroom, with a big mirror. He can be slow and phlegmatic in bed.

Sex showed in this card is pleasant, in a comfortable place, often in the bedroom where is a big mirror to be able to admire a lover during the sexual act. Long foreplay, with pleasant massage, surrounded by candles. Often, partners play role-playing and dress up in costumes.

Love

Upright:
relationship with a rich person, caring partner, trust, honesty, loyalty, fidelity, freedom, stable relationship, deep and lasting feelings, comfort

Reverse:
lack of trust, miserliness, greed, morbid jealousy, betrayal, insincerity, fear for the future of the relationship, suspicion

King of Pentacles

Sex

King of Pentacles describes a partner who is a very experienced lover, good lover, he knows how to give a pleasure to his partner, but sometimes he is selfish and cares only about his needs. Rather, he does not experiment, he sticks to what he knows and likes. He requires a lot from his partner and he prefers experienced and mature lovers.

Sex where a woman allows his partner to dominate her, in positions where a woman is focused to give a pleasure to a man. Without passions and experiments, there is also no deep emotions here.

In combination with 9 of Cups – oral sex
In combination with 9 of Pentacles or 6 of Pentacles - rich sponsor

Love

Upright:
solid and faithful partner, rich partner, stable relationship, material generosity, older partner, responsibility, calmness, future husband, a chance for long term relationship, ambition

Reverse:
relationship for money, being financially dependent on a partner, materialist, workaholic, bribery, egoism, loneliness, uncertain relationship, greedy partner, malignancy, dangerous lover, depravity

Spreads

The Next Lover.

1.   When You`ll meet your next partner/ lover?

2.   Where will you meet him/ her ?

3.   What will be his/hers physical appearance?

4.   What will be his/ her personality?

5.   What will be the future for this relationship?

What he/she likes?

1. What kind of lover is he/she?

2. What he/ she likes in bed?

3. What he/she does not like in sex?

How to diversify yours sexual life ?

1. What should you do to diversify yours sexual life?

2. What you should not to do?

3. How your partner will react to the proposed changes?

The Pleasure.

1. What do you think gives him pleasure?

2. What really gives him pleasure?

3. What is his most hidden fantasy?

4. What he does not consider, but it would give him pleasure?

5. Should you try to convince him to do it?

The Fears.

1. Which is the cause of his fears and blockades?

2. How can you overcome these blockades?

3. What should be done?

4. What should not be done?

5. What will be the effect of the actions taken?

What he/she secretly wishes?

1. Is he/she satisfied with your common sexual life?

2. What he/she secretly wishes?

3. What should you do to spice up your common sexual life?

The Date.

1. Will there be sex on this date?

2. Will he take the initiative?

3. Should you take the initiative?

What do you really like?

1. What he/she likes in bed?

2. What he/she does not like in sex?

3. What do you think he/she likes?

4. What does he/she think you like in bed?

5. What do you really like?

6. What you really do not like?

7. What should you try in bedroom?

Surprise me.

1. What will be this sex with him?

2. How he will surprise me?

3. How you will surprise him?

4. Will he do something that I do not like?

5. Will I do something that he does not like?

6. Will he be satisfied?

7. Will I be satisfied?

The Pregnancy

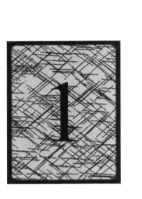

1. Will I have children with my partner?

2. Will there be problems with getting pregnant?

3. Does my partner want to have children?

4. What will be the gender of the first child?

Will your partner come back?

1. What are the partner's feelings for you at the moment?

2. Would he wish to come back to you?

3. What blocks him from returning?

4. What can you do to make your partner come back?

5. What should not be done?

6. The closest future of the relationship.

7. Will the partner come back to you?

First of all, thank you for purchasing this book. I hope it added at value and quality to your everyday life.

If so, it would be really nice if you could share this book with your friends and family by posting to Facebook, Twitter or Instagram.

I would like to hear from you and hope that you could take some time to post a review on Amazon.
Your feedback and support will help me to create future projects and make them even better.
Thank You!

Magdalene Aleece

Check the next page, a surprise is waiting for you!

Would you like to receive this beautiful Tarot Cheat Sheet ?

Contact me magdalenealeece@gmail.com , let me know when you bought my book and on which market (US, UK, DE etc) and I will send you 2 png files , 300 dpi, US letter size.

TAROT CHEAT SHEET — UPRIGHT MEANINGS

	Wands	Swords	Cups	Pentacles	The Major Arcana	
Ace	CREATION, NEW POSSIBILITIES, MOTIVATION, COURAGE, FERTILITY, INVENTION	ACTIVITY, OPPORTUNITY, DETERMINATION, INSPIRATION, EXAMS, JUSTICE	NEW LOVE, JOY, HAPPINESS, ABUNDANCE, NEW BEGINNING, OPPORTUNITY, FERTILITY	FRESH START, SUCCESS CHANCE, PROSPERITY, BEGINNING OF WEALTH	**The Fool** — FRESH HOPE, BEGINNING, FREEDOM, TRAVEL, NEW POSSIBILITIES	**The Justice** — DECISION MAKING, LOGIC, BALANCE, JUSTICE WILL BE DONE
2	MAKING PLANS, NEGOTIATIONS, FIRST STEP, REFLECTING ON ACTIONS	DUALITY, COMPROMISE, INDECISION, DIFFICULT DECISIONS, BEING BLIND TO SOMETHING, BLOCKAGE	ATTRACTION, BALANCE, COMPROMISE, BEGINNING OF FRIENDSHIP OR LOVE, AFFAIR, LOVE, JOY	MAKING A CHOICE, BALANCE, MESSAGES FROM FAR AWAY, PROPOSITION, TRADE	**The Magician** — BEGINNING, COMMUNICATION, DETERMINATION, CREATIVITY, INITIATIVE	**The Hanged Man** — CONTEMPLATION, WISDOM, WAITING, DELAY, A PAUSE IN ONE'S LIFE
3	REALIZATION OF HOPE, WEALTH, PARTNERSHIP, PATIENCE, ...	LOVE TRIANGLE, GREAT LOSS, PAIN, ...	FEAST, POSITIVE OUTCOME, SUCCESS, ABUNDANCE, ...	CREATIVITY, TRADE, INSPIRATION, MATERIAL INCREASE, ...	**The High Priestess**	**The Death** — TRANSFORMATION, PROGRESS, NEW

TAROT CHEAT SHEET — REVERSE MEANINGS

	Wands	Swords	Cups	Pentacles	The Major Arcana	
Ace	FALL, SEXUAL PROBLEMS, STAGNATION, RESTRICTIONS, FEAR OF CHANGES	SEXUAL PROBLEMS, BRUTALITY, OBSTACLES, GREAT LOSS, LACK OF CONCENTRATION	FALSE LOVE, SORROW, INSTABILITY, FEELING LOST, BREAKING PROMISES, LACK OF WILLINGNESS TO ACT	A FALSE START, GREED, LOSS, FAILURE, SUSPENSION OF ACTIONS	**The Fool** — MADNESS, RISK, CARELESSNESS, THOUGHTLESSNESS, UNFINISHED PROJECTS	**The Justice** — INJUSTICE, LEGAL COMPLICATIONS, SEPARATION, REVENGE, LIES
2	FEAR, PHYSICAL SUFFERING, RESTLESSNESS, HESITATION, NO AGREEMENT	BETRAYAL, DISLOYALTY, WRONG CHOICE, QUARRELS, AFFAIR	CONFUSION, LIES, SEPARATION, DISUNITY, FALSE LOVE, NO COMPROMISE, MISUNDERSTANDING	INDECISION, NO CHOICES LEFT, NO MESSAGES, NO CONTACT, SUSPENSION	**The Magician** — DOUBTS, SHYNESS, SELFISHNESS, DECEPTION, MANIPULATION	**The Hanged Man** — PUNISHMENT, WASTED EFFORT, ARROGANCE, DEFEAT, DISCOURAGEMENT
3	DECEPTION, MISTAKES, LOST PROJECTS, ISOLATION, DIFFICULTIES IN REALIZATION	REGRET, SORROW, AFFAIR, LESSER DEGREE OF LOSS AND PAIN (THAN IN UPRIGHT)	FEAR OF TAKING ACTION, MISSING OPPORTUNITIES, ISOLATION, OVERINDULGENCE	LOST CHANCES, LACK OF SKILLS, OBSTACLES, SELFISHNESS	**The High Priestess** — RESIGNATION, FEARS, SENSITIVENESS	**The Death** — DISASTER, LOSS, ILLNESS, FEARS, DEPRESSION

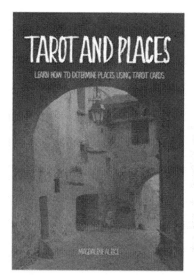

TAROT AND PLACES

Learn how to determine places using Tarot Cards

Magdalene Aleece

It is very difficult to determine a specific place with Tarot, but this short book will help you to get the answer for your questions;
Where will it happen ?
Where will we meet love ?
Where will be the first date with a new beloved ?

The author has been Tarot passionate for over 20 years and today shares her experience in this specific topic. In this book you will find a description of all 78 cards, so don't hesitate - take your cards, ask and finally get the answer!

52 Week Meal Planner

Victoria Mey

Kindle version - 20 pages (only Tips), Paperback version - 130 pages. (includes 52 week meal planner templates)
In kindle version of this title, you'll find tips about meal planning :
What is meal planning? Reasons to make a meal plan. How to create a meal plan that works. Extra tips to make your meal plan even better. What you can not freeze? Seasonal vegetables and fruits.
Kindle version doesn't include templates for meal planner for 52 weeks for obvious reason , but You'll find there example of templates included in paperback version, it may inspire you to create your own templates or let you see what templates you'll find in full paperback version!

Love is the most frequently occurring topic for which we ask Tarot cards, because who among us would not wish to know the answers to following questions:

Does he/she love me?

Will he invite me on a date?

Will he call me?

Will he/ she come back to me?

Will we get married?

In this little book you will find nearly forty spreads related to the theme of love.

Printed in Great Britain
by Amazon